JESUS IS ALIVE!

COLORING BOOK
WITH VERSES!

HOW TO DRAW

**Join today
for free puzzles!**

Join the Journey — Stay Connected!
I'd love to stay in touch with you.

Join my email list to receive **exclusive free printables, parenting resources**, sneak peeks at upcoming projects, and so much more!.
It's the best way to stay **connected** and inspired as we walk through this faith-filled journey together.

Let's passing foward the light of Jesus!
Many Blessing,
Stephanie Rodriguez

scan here

or go here

subscribepage.io/8IKeAC

JESUS CAME TO SAVE US!

"For God so loved the world..." – John 3:16

WE WERE LIKE LOST SHEEP

"We all, like sheep, have gone astray..."
— Isaiah 53:6

THE GOOD SHEPHERD FINDS HIS SHEEP

"I am the good shepherd." — John 10:11

JESUS LOVES ALL HIS CHILDREN

"Let the little children come to me."
– Matthew 19:14

JESUS HEALS US

"Little girl, I say to you, get up!"
— Mark 5:41

JESUS ON A DONKEY

"Blessed is He who comes
in the name of the Lord." — John 12:13

JESUS IS OUR KING!

The crowds shouted "Hosanna!"
(Which means: Save us!) — Matthew 21:9

LAST SUPPER
WITH HIS FRIENDS

"...I have called you friends, for everything that I learned from my Father I have made known to you." - John 15:15

PRAYING IN THE GARDEN

Not my will, but yours be done."
— Luke 22:42

HE DIED ON THE CROSS FOR ME

But God shows his love for us in this:
While we were still sinners, Christ died for us. Romans 5:8

THIS IS HOW HE SAVED US

"For God so loved the world…" — John 3:16

JESUS WAS BURIED

"They laid Him in a tomb." — Luke 23:53

EARTHQUAKE!!

"Suddenly there was a great earthquake"
-Matthew 28:2

THE TOMB IS EMPTY WHERE IS JESUS?

"The stone had been rolled away." — Mark 16:4

HE IS NOT HERE JESUS IS ALIVE!

"He is not here; He has risen!" — Luke 24:6

JESUS APPEARS TO MARY

"I have seen the Lord!" – John 20:18

JESUS APPEARS TO HIS DISCIPLES

"Peace be with you." — John 20:19

JESUS SENDS HIS FRIENDS TO TELL OTHERS

"Go and tell everyone the good news."
—Mark 16:15

JESUS GOES BACK TO HEAVEN

"He was taken up into heaven."
— Luke 24:51

JESUS WILL COME BACK!

will come back in the same way you have seen him go into heaven."— Acts 1:11

JESUS LIVES
IN OUR HEARTS

"I am with you always." — Matthew 28:20

FOLLOW THE STEPS:

DRAW THE BABY CHICK

DRAW HERE

DRAW THE SHEEP

DRAW HERE

FOLLOW THE STEPS:

DRAW THE PORCUPINE

DRAW HERE

DRAW THE BUNNY

DRAW HERE

FOLLOW THE STEPS:

DRAW THE TURTLE

DRAW HERE

DRAW THE SQUIRREL

DRAW HERE

FOLLOW THE STEPS:

DRAW THE DONKEY

DRAW HERE

DRAW THE BOY

DRAW HERE

FOLLOW THE STEPS:

DRAW THE RED PANDA

DRAW HERE

DRAW THE ANGEL

DRAW HERE

ENJOYED THE BOOK?
WE'D LOVE YOUR FEEDBACK!

THE BEST WAY TO SUPPORT OUR MINISTRY:
1. **SHARE** THIS BOOK WITH A FRIEND
2. **LEAVE ME A REVIEW** ON AMAZON
THANK YOU!